I0163733

Punching Holes: Buying Ammunition, Gun Accessories, Knives and Tactical Gear at Wholesale Prices

TYLER CAPOBRES

Copyright © 2017 by Tyler Capobres

All rights reserved. No part of this
publication may be reproduced, distributed,
or transmitted in any form or by any means,
including photocopying, recording, or other
electronic or mechanical methods, without
the prior written permission of the publisher,
except in the case of brief quotations
embodied in critical reviews and certain
other noncommercial uses permitted by
copyright law. For permission requests,
write to the publisher, addressed "Attention:
Permissions Coordinator," at the address
below.

Printed in the United States of America

Tyler Capobres

ISBN 978-0-9997782-0-3

Table of Contents

Introduction

If you're like me, you're a gun owner. We buy guns, and spend even more money customizing them. I have one shotgun that cost nearly $2000 once I was finished customizing it how I wanted. Don't forget you'll also need ammunition for those guns. If you're lucky, your local retailer might have a few boxes on the shelf. If not, you have to start calling around or buy it online. Next, you'll want some more magazines, speed loaders and additional equipment, because nobody wants to spend half their day at the range reloading. Add it all up and you're paying an arm and a leg to various retailers for all the guns, ammunition and gear you want.

What if I told you that you've been going about it all wrong this whole time? Would you believe me if I told you I was in the same boat, until I found a way to save 15-40% by buying it at wholesale prices? Whether you believe me or not, I've done it. I've purchased $145 60-round AR15 magazines for $110. I've purchased name brand optics for $70 cheaper than the lowest online prices. If you're willing to put in some time and effort, it will pay off dividends.

Chapter 1 – Benefits of Buying Wholesale

I have worked in retail before, and I can assure you that there isn't much markup being added onto ammunition and guns themselves, but gun accessories and tactical gear are a different story. You can expect a minimum markup of 15-20% on most items, and that doesn't include sales tax. That may not seem like much to you, but it certainly adds up. Let's say you buy a pair of ear muffs for $19.98. Assuming the markup is "only" 20%, that's $3.33 you're giving to the retailer. On top of that, you're paying sales tax on the retail value of the item. Where I live that's an additional 6%, so add another $1.20. You're now paying $4.52 more, which you could've spent on something else, or just saved the money for later. It doesn't seem like much, but when you add up all the purchases you make in a week, month, year, etc., I think you'd be surprised at how much you're giving to the retailers.

While online retailers try to lower the cost of shipping, they can only go so far before it starts uncomfortably cutting into their profits. Yes, there are websites that will offer free shipping if you order over a certain dollar amount, but I've never had luck finding a one-stop-shop website where I could combine ammunition, gun accessories and tactical gear into one purchase.

Some wholesalers will offer you flat-rate

shipping. There's one I use that charges me $9 to ship practically whatever I want. No, I haven't tried ordering an entire pallet of ammunition, but I have ordered several magazines, several boxes of ammunition and a knife or two. Care to guess what I paid for shipping? You guessed it: $9. Even while writing this book, I received an email from one of the companies I purchase from, informing me that shipping has been reduced. Ground shipping is now $9.95, and only $14.95 for 2nd Day Air.

Sometimes you'll find shipping costs are cheaper ordering online, than through wholesale channels. There have been a number of occasions where I found myself in such a situation, and ended up purchasing through retail channels because it ended up saving me a few dollars over wholesale costs. When you see those opportunities, take them.

Shipping costs really come into play

when you combine them with larger inventory selection. One dealer I use has average shipping costs, which sometimes end up being more expensive than through retail channels, but their selection is what keeps me coming back. In one order I can purchase a 50rd drum magazine for my Ruger 10/22, 1.25" 12-gauge buckshot, hearing protection, magazines and any upgrades or gun replacement parts I want. Their inventory is so large that I can do that, whereas elsewhere it would require me to pay 4-5 different retailers to buy the same things. I'd also have to pay shipping costs to each retailer, which would set me back anywhere from $30-50. It's cases like these where a large inventory, combined with discounted or flat-rate shipping, allows you to make your money go further.

Chapter 2 – Show Me The Savings!

Now that I have your attention, I'm sure you're curious just how much I've saved using this system. Let me show you some examples. For purposes of simplification, I am only comparing the savings without shipping charges.

Ammunition

Interestingly enough, this category has the least savings involved, depending on the type of ammunition you buy. While I did save some money over places like Ammo Seek, there are often times online deals that cannot be beaten.

Speer Gold Dot 9mm 124GR 20rds per box

Retail: $21.00

Wholesale: $18.79

Savings: $2.21 (10% savings)

American Eagle 5.56 XM193 150rds per box

Retail: $52.97

Wholesale: $46.44

Savings: $6.53 (12% savings)

Gun Accessories

This is the largest area where you will save a lot of money buying at wholesale prices. The markup on these items can easily be double what you pay at wholesale.

GSG 22LR 110rd Drum Magazine for Ruger 10/22

Retail: $67.53

Wholesale: $39.95

Savings: $27.58 (40% savings)

Lula Loader for AK47/Galil

Retail: $26.95

Wholesale: $19.11

Savings: $7.84 (29% savings)

Smith & Wesson Shield 9mm 8rd Magazine

Retail: $33.59

Wholesale: $27.09

Savings: $6.50 (19% savings)

Surefire AR-15 60rd Magazine

Retail: $129

Wholesale: $90.30

Savings: $38.70 (30% savings)

Guns

While I haven't purchased any guns personally, I will use my personal favorite handgun, the Walther PPQ M2, as an example. When I first purchased this gun, it cost me $600.

Walther PPQ M2 4" 9mm

Retail: $600

Wholesale: $511

Savings: $99 (16% savings)

Obviously, the savings you get depend on the manufacturer, popularity, demand, etc. Due to length, I haven't listed all of the purchases I've made using this system. After going through invoices, I calculated I had spent $480.88 on ammunition and gun accessories. Using the same method above, I came up with the following:

Retail: $599.48

Wholesale: $480.88

Savings: $118.60 (19% savings overall)

Now you've seen the markup retailers are charging that you could be saving. I'm not demonizing retailers by any means. They provide an important service for our communities, and their desire to make a profit isn't wrong. Our society thrives on capitalism and I wouldn't have it any other way. My system will walk you through how to create your own business with your state, apply for sales and use permits, and start setting up wholesale dealer accounts so you can start saving money.

Chapter 3 – Getting Your DBA/ABN

To do business in my state, you're required to register a DBA (Doing Business As) or ABN (Assumed Business Name) through the office of the Secretary of State. The fastest way to locate the website is to search for it on a major search engine, using the phrase "secretary of state + [your state]". Once you find the website, I was able to locate the necessary forms under the "Business Entities" section of the left-hand menu. There should be a link titled

"Assumed Business Names", "Doing Business As" or something similar to the two, where you can view and print off the necessary application forms. This section should also list the fees involved for filing, which will need to be paid by a check enclosed with your application. My state has no issue with multiple ABNs with the same names, but your state's policy may differ. If it does differ, there should be a notice provided on the page. If there isn't, call and verify before mailing your application. Lastly, I highly recommend acquiring a PO Box through the post office, or something similar through a UPS or FedEx location. Your business's address will be public record, so I opted for an additional layer of privacy.

Some states will also require there be a public announcement published in the local newspaper, which will list your personal and business name. If they do not offer such a service, you should be able to request an ad by contacting your local newspaper. If instructions on the agency's website are vague, do not hesitate to call them and ask for clarification. When the announcement appears in the paper, I recommend making a copy of it and retaining it as proof. It's always better to have more paperwork than less.

I received my official certificate in the mail after approximately two weeks. While it shouldn't take longer, do not be surprised if it does. You can always call and verify your application was received, and ask for the status of the application. Once your certificate arrives, keep it in a safe place. You will need this document as proof for later in this process. Lastly, be aware of any renewal requirements for your DBA/ABN. While my state does not require a renewal, and simply lets it continue into perpetuity until I cancel it, not all state agencies will handle it in this same manner.

Chapter 4 – Sales and Use Permits

Once you have your DBA/ABN certificate in hand, you are ready to apply for a sales and/or use permit. This should be conducted through your state's tax commission. As mentioned earlier, it's easiest to search for their website on a major search engine, using the search phrase "state tax commission + [your state]". For me, the link to apply for permits was all located under the "Online Services" link. If your state's tax commission has no such category, look for a "Business" section.

My state gives the option of filing electronically or via mail, so I chose to submit my application online. The application starts out asking about your type of business, its purpose, and which permits you are seeking. Make sure you check the "Use" box, and also check the "Sales" box if you plan to sell. If pursuing this as a business, you will want to provide a Federal EIN (Employer Identification Number). If you are only doing this for personal use, provide your personal SSN. You will then provide your ABN and list the date of incorporation as the day your ABN was approved.

The remaining boxes are self-explanatory, until you come to the section asking about the "primary nature of business". Honesty is always the best course of action, so under "Primary

Business Function" I put "Other Direct Selling Establishments", since I would be purchasing from wholesalers exclusively. Under "Primary Business Function Description" I put "The business is to purchase ammunition at wholesale cost for personal use and retail sales". After listing the names of all owners, their SSN and related information, they'll have you proceed through additional questions that relate to employees, wages, unemployment taxes, etc. If you're pursuing this for personal use only, this section is fairly quick to fill out. Once you're done with this, sign and date the application and submit it. I was approved and received my permit in about two weeks.

Depending on the state, a Sales Permit can be a separate license you must apply for, or can be combined into a Sales AND Use Permit. For example, while I checked off both the "Use" and "Sales" boxes on the application, my state only issues a Sales Permit and expects me to make the necessary use tax payments in addition to any sales tax.

Chapter 5 – Acquiring Wholesale Accounts

This is the part I'm sure you've been waiting for this whole time. Now it's time to start signing up for wholesale dealer accounts with various companies. The easiest way to find these companies is to do a simple search for them. If you're not having any luck there, don't be afraid to visit various firearms message boards and search through their posts. The collective knowledge on some of these message boards is extremely impressive.

If you don't plan on applying for an FFL to sell guns, you'll want to avoid the wholesalers who only sell to those with an FFL. While I disagree with their decision to do so, I can assure you they will not budge from it. You'll be happy to know that there are still a number of wholesalers who don't have that requirement, so not all is lost. If you do have an FFL or are planning to get one, this will be covered in detail in the following chapter.

When you find some wholesalers that interest you, look for a link that says "Become A Dealer", or something along those lines. If you come across a company's website and it doesn't have a link referencing becoming a dealer, don't be afraid to call or email them to find out. They'll have you fill out a form with all the information pertaining to your business, and will want you to upload a scanned copy of your DBA/ABN and Sales/Use Permit. If they have a section asking what your plans are, be completely honest with them. Most companies don't mind if you're mainly buying for yourself, friends, and only occasionally (or never) selling to others. Remember, they make a profit even if you don't turn around and resell it to someone else, so you're not going to hurt their feelings one bit.

Once your account is approved, make sure you reset your password. Typically, it's automatically generated, and not very easy to remember. In the email you receive, check to see if you have been assigned a particular sales representative. While you're more than welcome to call their customer service number, it's much more beneficial to establish a relationship with your assigned sales representative. Next, go through and update your contact information. Some wholesalers will require a sales representative contact you before finalizing any orders. Most don't require this, but it's still good to keep all of your information current.

Chapter 6 – Finding Good Wholesalers

Finding good wholesalers can take hours to research and find. The easiest method is finding firearms message boards and forums, and searching for information on wholesalers. To help get you started, I've provided a list of known wholesalers. The list is broken down into wholesalers who primarily sell guns and require an FFL, and those who don't require an FFL.

It should be noted that wholesalers

marked with an * are ones I've used personally and recommend. Those without an * come recommended from others, and I recommend doing your own research to decide if they're the right fit for you.

FFL Required

- Lipsey's - www.lipseys.com
- Davidson's - www.davidsonsinc.com
- Zander's Sporting Goods - www.gzanders.com

No FFL Required

- MGE Wholesale -

www.mgewholesale.com

- Williams Shooters Supply - www.willshoot.com

- Crow Shooting Supply* - www.crowshootingsupply.com

- Chattanooga Shooting Supplies* - www.chattanoogashooting.com

- RSR Group* - www.rsrgroup.com

FFL Exception

While you can't order firearms without an FFL, I have confirmed with both RSR and Chattanooga that this only applies to firearms with a serial number. Since the lower receiver of an AR15 is considered the actual firearm component, both wholesalers will ship any parts and complete uppers directly to you. While this does limit your options, it does give you some additional cost savings if you've ever wanted a different caliber, such as 300 Blackout or 458 SOCOM, in an AR platform.

The process of purchasing from a wholesaler varies. When going through Chattanooga or RSR, the process is almost identical to online shopping, save for additional payment options and terms. While RSR purchases are completely automated, not all are. Crow Shooting Supply and Chattanooga Shooting Supply require a salesperson to confirm the order with you before it is finalized, so expect a slight delay. Each wholesaler has its trade-offs, but is beneficial in its own way.

Chapter 7 – How to Order

Chattanooga Shooting Supplies

Chattanooga is one of the wholesalers I use regularly, due to their large variety of inventory in guns, ammunition, gun accessories and tactical gear. To help with ordering for the first time, I thought a short guide might make your first purchase go smoothly.

Before placing an order, be sure to read the "Company Policies" section of the website, located under the main "Company Info" link. There are strict rules to be followed when returning merchandise, and extra fees are added on if your order is less than $25 and $50. If you're aware of the rules you can still save a lot of money. If you're not aware of them, what should've been a savings could result in an inflated final bill.

Once you've successfully logged into the website, you can use the navigation on the left-hand side of the site to find what you're looking for by category. If you have a specific group of items or single item in mind, it's faster to use the search function. The major downside to searching through multiple pages of merchandise is the site lacks the ability to sort by price, relevance, ratings, etc. If you already know what you want, the search function is your friend. If you're browsing through their catalog to find something interesting, be sure to reserve a good portion of time, since their inventory is unbelievably large.

Once you've added the items to the cart and checked out, be prepared to wait one or two business days. The reason for this is so a salesperson can review the order, shipping fees can be finalized, and any extra fees can be included in the final price.

RSR Group

Unlike Chattanooga, RSR is easier to shop with since their system allows you to sort by price. There are no minimum fees with RSR, but the same merchandise carried between them and Chattanooga is sometimes more expensive through RSR.

The ordering process is similar up to a point, until it comes time to check out. Once the item is in your cart, click the "Checkout" button. After clicking the button, the inventory will be reserved for 10 minutes. This is an extra feature I like to use when I'm searching for an item that isn't commonly stocked or is in extremely high demand. Once you're ready to pay, fill in your payment information, click "Final Submit" and your order is complete.

Chapter 8 – Buying Guns Wholesale

Probably the most-sought-after portion of this book will be in this chapter. It's also in this chapter that I must warn you about the requirements that must be met before you can enjoy discounts on gun purchases. You will not only have to meet the criteria required by the ATF, but also those of the wholesalers themselves.

As of February 17, 2017, the ATF has ruled that an applicant may sell exclusively at gun shows, through the internet and by mail, and does not have to exclusively sell guns from their premises. This means you are not obligated to have a retail storefront to be in the business of selling guns. Be aware that this is ultimately at their discretion, and could change at any time.

While the ATF doesn't have an issue with a person selling guns without a retail storefront, this isn't necessarily the case for wholesalers. Some companies will also want proof of a retail storefront. Without a retail storefront, a large portion of wholesalers will not sell you guns. I am unaware of these companies' stance on selling guns out of a leased office space, so I would encourage you to verify with the wholesaler before considering looking into leasing. While it may not seem like much of an inconvenience, it is certainly something to consider when weighing the benefits vs drawbacks of trying to purchase guns at wholesale prices.

Chapter 9 – Buying Knives Wholesale

If you're like me and also enjoy a good knife, sword, tomahawk and the like, you'll happy to know you can save money on all of these as well. If you recall the list of wholesalers in Chapter 6, the two main wholesalers I work with are Chattanooga Shooting Supplies and RSR Group. In addition to having a large selection of guns, accessories, gear and ammo, they also have a sizable selection of knives.

Both Chattanooga and RSR boast 16 pages of name-brand knives at prices even Amazon can't beat. They also have you covered if you need a sheath, sharpening tools, cases and more.

The last wholesaler I have only dealt with once. They are reputable and have incredible prices on name-brand knives. They certainly have the best prices of all the wholesalers, but you will want to make sure you read the caveats I've listed in the next couple paragraphs.

● Blue Ridge Knives

http://www.blueridgeknives.com

When I started looking for knife wholesalers, I came across many that were willing to sell lots of cheap, off-brand knives. So far, Blue Ridge Knives is the only exception I've found. I've also personally ordered from them, and can confidently say they are the real deal. Most of their knives are at least 25% off retail, with some selling for as little as 50% off retail pricing.

I will caution you that they claim you must make at least one purchase every 6 months to continue having dealer access. There is a minimum purchase order of $100. In addition, your total purchases with them must be at least $500 per year, although I can't find that information anywhere in their policies.

Most people don't spend $500 in knives each year. I replied to their email, notifying them I would be unable to meet these qualifications and to cancel my account so as to not waste their time. I never heard back from them. My account will most likely be canceled at the end of 6 months,

since I simply don't buy knives that
frequently.

Chapter 10 – Sales and Use Taxes

Now that you have your business set up, the proper permits and some wholesale accounts to purchase from, it's time to talk about what everyone dreads: taxes. All businesses are required to pay sales or use tax. Whether you're buying or selling, the government will want its cut. While the rate is typically the same, you will want to know which category of taxes you fall under.

Sales Tax

If you plan on running a business, you will want a sales permit to operate legally within the state. You will need to collect sales tax for all sales, in addition to filing regular income tax. You'll want to set an appropriate portion of profits aside to pay for Social Security taxes, which a normal employer takes out of a paycheck on behalf of an employee. It's best to consult the IRS website, in addition to an experienced CPA, to avoid nasty letters and penalties.

Use Tax

If you plan on simply purchasing guns, ammunition, knives and gear for yourself, you'll pay a use tax. The use tax is typically the same rate as sales tax, and is paid for anything that is used or stored, but never sold.

Chapter 11 – Tracking and Paying Your Taxes

Once you've received your Sales Permit and/or Use Permit, you will be told how frequently sales and use taxes will be due. In general, your state's tax commission will most likely have you file quarterly. You will receive a notice in the mail, along with instructions on how to paper file. If your state is like mine, you'll also have the more convenient option of filing online through the state tax commission's website. This will allow you to pay any taxes via ACH withdrawal, check or credit card.

Unlike income taxes the form is relatively short, and typically takes 10 minutes to file and pay any taxes owed. For my state's online return form, there are 12 boxes, most of which I leave blank. The only box I fill out is for the total dollar amount (including shipping) of all purchases made for personal use.

While it's unlikely you'll have the state tax commission audit you, it's always a possibility. For that reason, it's best to keep excellent records of all purchases you've made, whether for personal use or resale. You will be taxed on the full amount of your purchase, including shipping, so you don't need to worry about having a complex spreadsheet to keep track of it all. Simply having a few columns indicating the purchase date, company purchased from and the purchase total should be sufficient. For more detailed records you can simply log into your account and retrieve any further details.

In the event you miss your tax payment deadline, don't panic. If you don't owe any taxes, there usually isn't a late penalty. If you do owe taxes, don't be surprised if you're hit with a $10-15 late penalty, plus a percentage of your outstanding tax balance. It's not fun and these things happen sometimes, but it's best to simply pay the fine and move on. It's usually not worth the time and money to challenge them on it.

Make sure you fully understand your state's expectations regarding reporting, filing and paying your taxes. My experience may not be the same as yours. If you have the slightest doubt or concern, take the time to contact your state's tax commissions and ask for clarification.

Chapter 12 – Business Potential

By now you're probably wondering about the viability of using this system to run a business. With a solid business plan, you very might well establish a loyal customer base and make some money, whether you decide to sell in-person, online or in a retail storefront.

Drop Shipping

One distinct advantage to some of the wholesale accounts is you can have them create a customer drop shipping account. This means customers place their order, you accept payment, then pay the wholesaler to drop ship the items to the customer's address. This method has its advantages by reducing shipping costs. It also has the disadvantage of requiring extra steps for the customer, which not all will want to do for every single order.

Pricing

Most of the time you will be able to beat the competition in pricing. The exceptions to this are typically with ammunition and guns, where the margins are incredibly slim. You'll also want to pay attention to pricing agreements, since some products are not allowed to be advertised below a specific price. Spyderco and SOG do this frequently. One way around it is to simply put "Add to cart to see price", "Contact for pricing" or "Too low to show". This allows you to offer the products at a lower price, since you're not advertising the lower price.

Inventory

Another advantage you will have over other competitors is the large selection of inventory available to you. The only disadvantage to this is you can occasionally run into a situation where the products the customer wants are through different wholesalers.

Automatic Drop Shipping

Some third-party companies offer services where you can directly implement the various wholesalers' inventories into an e-commerce website. You control how much profit you want, and their software takes care of customer accounts and orders from start to finish. You collect the profits and the wholesalers drop ship to your customers with your address, so you never have to touch the merchandise. I have yet to delve into these, so be extremely cautious and do your research. Some wholesalers have official partners who will do this, but their monthly fees are usually much higher.

Advertising

The biggest disadvantage will be advertising, whether it's online, in-person or in a retail location. Online is exceptionally challenging, since the cost to enter the market is relatively low. The majority of the cost will be in attracting customers to the website.

With in-person sales, it's crucial you build a reputation. Word-of-mouth is key, and advertising can still help you here as well. While your dealings may be face-to-face, you have a greater reach through message boards, forums, Facebook groups, etc.

Retail Storefront

The largest cost of all is setting up your own retail storefront. In addition to the initial setup costs, you'll want to consider the overhead costs for utilities, employees, rent, etc., and plan at least five years out. The most common reasons small businesses fail are poor planning and cash flow issues. If done right, you could build a large business that offers customers quality merchandise at affordable prices.

A retail storefront is the one exception where you can make money on ammunition. Normally the margins are too low to beat online prices. With a retail store, customers are more likely to purchase at higher prices if they're already buying something else from you.

Conclusion

Hopefully this book hasn't been too overwhelming or complicated. It seems that way at first, but I promise the benefits are certainly worth it in the long-run. There's a great satisfaction from knowing you aren't dependent on local retailers, Amazon, Midway, Brownells, etc., for ammunition, guns, accessories and gear. It's also much easier to find products you didn't know existed, such as a 110-round drum magazine for the Ruger 10/22.

The most important aspect I can't stress enough is to make sure you pay your taxes. Always round up, never down. The last headache you want in your life is an audit, so make sure your records are accurate and pay taxes on everything, including shipping costs. Saving 15-40% or more is certainly worth the small price you'll pay in taxes.

I started this whole process purely in it for myself and saving money. Over time, I came to realize this information is simply too good to not share with others. Sure, the retailers and even some wholesalers may hate me for it, but I couldn't care less. If you're reading this book, you're just like me. Money doesn't grow on trees, so saving every little bit helps. Hopefully this book helps you save a fortune over your lifetime. If it helped you in any way, please don't hesitate to share it with someone else. Happy savings!

About The Author

Tyler Capobres wasn't introduced to guns until he was 18, and is quickly making up for lost time. He was first published in a Yu-Gi-Oh trading card game magazine at the age of 15. He is the author of a children's book, *Tall Tales from Nesbit Elementary*.

In 2013, he started publishing product reviews on YouTube (www.youtube.com/dstedunet) that are short, honest, and test each product's endurance. He continues educating people through his personal website, The Good Gun (www.thegoodgun.com). If he's not testing products, exotic ammunition, or sending lead downrange, you can find him on his personal blog at www.tylercapobres.com.

www.ingramcontent.com/pod-product-compliance
Lightning Source LLC
Chambersburg PA
CBHW060610030426
42337CB00018B/3030